Affiliate Marketing A-Z!

Easy Steps to Maximize Your Potential

**from the library of the
New Thrive Learning Institute**

Get Related Materials

from Our Free Library

Instant Access – Join Here

Click or type into your browser:

http://livesensical.com/go/byob/

LEGAL NOTICE:

Table of Contents

Introduction..3
3 Things All Affiliate Marketers Need To Survive Online..6
Top 3 Ways To Boost Your Affiliate Commissions
Overnight...9
Which Affiliate Networks To Look Out For When
Promoting...12
So Many Affiliate Programs! Which One Do I Choose?...15
Here's How To Avoid The 3 Most Common Affiliate
Mistakes...17
Using Product Recommendations To Increase Your
Bottom Line..20
Easy Profits Using PPC In Your Affiliate Marketing
Business..23
Using Camtasia Can Increase Your Affiliate Checks........26
How To Become A Super Affiliate In Niche Markets.......29
Resources..32

Introduction

Being in the affiliate marketing business is not that hard now with the Internet at your disposable. It is much easier now compared to the days when people have to make use of the telephones and other mediums of information just to get the latest updates on the way their program is coming along.

So with technology at hand, and assuming that the affiliate is working from home, a day in his or her life would sound something like this...

Upon waking up and after having breakfast, the computer is turned on to check out new developments in the network. As far as the marketer is concerned there might be new things to update and statistics to keep track on.

The site design has to be revised. The marketer knows that a well-designed site can increase sign ups from visitors. It can also help in the affiliate's conversion rates.

That done, it is time to submit the affiliate program to directories that lists affiliate programs. These directories are means to attract people in joining your affiliate program. A sure way of promoting the affiliate program.

Time to track down the sales you are getting from your affiliates fairly and accurately. There are phone orders and mails to track down.

See if they are new clients checking the products out. Noting down the contact information that might be a viable source in the future.

There are lots of resources to sort out. Ads, banners, button ads and sample recommendations to give out because the marketer knows that this is one way of ensuring more sales. Best to stay visible and accessible too.

The affiliate marketer remembered that there are questions to answer from the visitors. This has to be done quickly. Nothing can turn off a customer than an unanswered email.

To prove that the affiliate is working effectively and efficiently, inquiries would have to be paid more attention on. Nobody wants to be ignored and customers are not always the most patient of all people. Quick answer that should appear professional yet friendly too.

In the process of doing all the necessities, the marketer is logged on to a chat room where he or she interacts with other affiliates and those under that same program. This is where they can discuss things on how to best promote their products.

There are things to be learned and it is a continuous process. Sharing tips and advices is a good way of showing support. There may be others out there wanting to join and may be enticed by the discussion that is going on. There is no harm in assuming what opportunities ahead.

The newsletters and ezines were updated days ago, so it is time for the affiliate marketer to see if there are some new things happening in the market. This will be written about in the marketer's publication to be distributed to the old and new customers.

These same publications are also an important tool in keeping up to date with the newly introduced products. The marketer has put up a sale and promotion that customers may want to know about. Besides, they have to keep up with the deadline of these sales written in the publications.

Affiliate Marketing A to Z - 5

It is that time to show some appreciation to those who have helped the marketer in the promotions and sale increase. Nothing like mentioning the persons, their sites and the process they have done that made everything worked.

Of course, this will be published in the newsletters. Among the more important information that have been written already.

The marketer still has time to write out recommendations to those who want credible sources for the products being promoted. There is also time to post some comments on how to be a successful affiliate marketer on a site where there are lots of wannabes.

Two objectives done at the same time. The marketer gets to promote the product as well as the program they are in. Who knows, someone may be inclined to join.

Time flies. Missed lunch but is quite contented with the tasks done. Bed time....

Ok, so this may not be all done in a day. But then, this gives you an idea of how an affiliate marketer, a dedicated one that is, spends the marketing day.

Is that success looming in the distance or what?

3 Things All Affiliate Marketers Need To Survive Online

Every affiliate marketer is always looking for the successful market that gives the biggest paycheck. Sometimes they think it is a magic formula that is readily available for them. Actually, it is more complicated than that. It is just good marketing practices that have been proven over years of hard work and dedication.

There are tactics that have worked before with online marketing and is continuing to work in the online affiliate marketing world of today. With these top three marketing tips, you will be able to able to increase your sales and survive in the affiliate marketing online.

What are these three tactics?

1. Using unique web pages to promote each separate product you are marketing. Do not lump all of it together just to save some money on web hosting. It is best to have a site focusing on each and every product and nothing more.

Always include product reviews on the website so visitors will have an initial understanding on what the product can do to those who buys them. Also include testimonials from users who have already tried the product.

Be sure that these customers are more than willing to allow you to use their names and photos on the site of the specific product you are marketing.

You can also write articles highlighting the uses of the product and include them on the website as an additional page. Make the pages attractive compelling and include calls to act on the information. Each headline should attract the readers to try and read more, even contact you. Highlight your special points. This will help your readers to learn what the page is about and will want to find out more.

2. Offer free reports to your readers. If possible position them at the very top side of your page so it they simply cannot be missed. Try to create autoresponder messages that will be mailed to those who input their personal information into your sign up box. According to research, a sale is closed usually on the seventh contact with a prospect.

Only two things can possibly happen with the web page alone: closed sale or the prospect leaving the page and never return again. By placing useful information into their inboxes at certain specified period, you will remind them of the product they thought they want later and will find out that the sale is closed. Be sure that the content is directed toward specific reasons to buy the product. Do not make it sound like a sales pitch.

Focus on important points like how your product can make life and things easier and more enjoyable. Include compelling subject lines in the email. As much as possible, avoid using the word "free" because there are still older spam filters that dumps those kind of contents into the junk before even anyone reading them first. Convince those who signed up for your free reports that they will be missing something big if they do not avail of your products and services.

3. Get the kind of traffic that is targeted to your product. Just think, if the person who visited your website has no interest whatsoever in what you are offering, they will be among those who move on and never come back. Write articles for publication in e-zines and e-reports. This way you can locate

publications that is focusing on your target customers and what you have put up might just grab their interest.

Try to write a minimum of 2 articles per week, with at least 300-600 words in length.

By continuously writing and maintaining these articles you can generate as many as 100 targeted readers to your site in a day.

Always remember that only 1 out of 100 people are likely to buy your product or get your services. If you can generate as much as 1,000 targeted hits for your website in a day, that means you can made 10 sales based on the average statistic.

The tactics given above does not really sound very difficult to do, if you think about it. It just requires a little time and an action plan on your part.

Try to use these tips for several affiliate marketing programs. You can end maintaining a good source of income and surviving in this business that not all marketers can do.

Besides, think of the huge paychecks you will be receiving...

Top 3 Ways To Boost Your Affiliate Commissions Overnight

The ideal world of affiliate marketing does not require having your won website, dealing with customers, refunds, product development and maintenance. This is one of the easiest ways of launching into an online business and earning more profits.

Assuming you are already into an affiliate program, what would be the next thing you would want to do? Double, or even triple, your commissions, right? How do you do that?

Here are some powerful tips on how to boost your affiliate program commissions overnight.

1. Know the best program and products to promote. Obviously, you would want to promote a program that will enable you to achieve the greatest profits in the shortest possible time.

There are several factors to consider in selecting such a program. Choose the ones that have a generous commission structure. Have products that fit in with your target audience. And that has a solid track record of paying their affiliate easily and on time. If you cannot seem to increase your investments, dump that program and keep looking for better ones.

There are thousands of affiliate programs online which gives you the reason to be picky. You may want to select the best to avoid losing your advertising dollars.

Write free reports or short ebooks to distribute from your site. There is a great possibility that you are competing with other affiliates that are promoting the same program. If you start writing short report related to the product you are promoting, you will be able to distinguish yourself from the other affiliates.

In the reports, provide some valuable information for free. If possible, add some recommendations about the products. With ebooks, you get credibility. Customers will see that in you and they will be enticed to try out what you are offering.

2. Collect and save the email addresses of those who download your free ebooks. It is a known fact that people do not make a purchase on the first solicitation. You may want to send out your message more than six times to make a sale.

This is the simple reason why you should collect the contact information of those who downloaded your reports and ebooks. You can make follow-ups on these contacts to remind them to make a purchase from you.

Get the contact information of a prospect before sending them to the vendor's website. Keep in mind that you are providing free advertisement for the product owners. You get paid only when you make a sale. If you send prospects directly to the vendors, chances are they would be lost to you forever.

But when you get their names, you can always send other marketing messages to them to be able to earn an ongoing commission instead of a one-time sale only.

Publish an online newsletter or Ezine. It is always best to recommend a product to someone you know than to sell to a stranger. This is the purpose behind publishing your own newsletter. This also allows you to develop a relationship based on trust with your subscribers.

This strategy is a delicate balance between providing useful information with a sales pitch. If you continue to write informative editorials you will be able to build a sense of reciprocity in your readers that may lead them to support you by buying your products.

3. Ask for higher than normal commission from merchants. If you are already successful with a particular promotion, you should try and approach the merchant and negotiate a percentage commission for your sales.

If the merchant is smart, he or she will likely grant your request rather than lose a valuable asset in you. Keep in mind that you are a zero-risk investment to your merchant; so do not be shy about requesting for addition in your commissions. Just try to be reasonable about it.

Write strong pay Per Click ads. PPC search engine is the most effective means of advertising online. As an affiliate, you can make a small income just by managing PPC campaigns such as Google AdWords and Overture. Then you should try and monitor them to see which ads are more effective and which ones to dispose of.

Try out these strategies and see the difference it can make to your commission checks in the shortest of time.

Which Affiliate Networks To Look Out For When Promoting

There are many horror stories about affiliate programs and networks. People have heard them over and over again, that some are even wary of joining one. The stories they may have heard are those related to illegal programs or pyramid schemes. Basically, this kind of market does not have real, worthy product.

You do not want to be associated with these schemes. It is obvious you want to be with a program that offers high quality product that you will readily endorse. The growing number of those who have joined already and are succeeding immensely is proof enough that there are reliable and quality affiliate programs out there.

Why participate in an affiliate program?

It allows you to work part-time. It gives you the opportunity to build a generous residual income. And it makes you an owner of a small business. Affiliate programs have already created lots of millionaires. They are the living testimony of how hard work; continuous prospecting, motivating and training others pay off.

If ever you are deciding to join one, you must take note that you are getting into something that is patterned to what you are capable of.

This will be an assurance that you are capable of doing anything to come out successful.

How do you choose a good affiliate program to promote? Here are some tips you may want to look over before choosing one:

- A program that you like and have interest in. One of the best ways of knowing if that is the kind of program you wish to promote is if you are interested in purchasing the product yourself. If that is the case, chances are, there are many others who are also interested in the same program and products.

- Look for a program that is of high quality. For instance, look for one that is associated with many experts in that particular industry. This way, you are assured that of the standard of the program you will be joining into.

- Join in the ones that offer real and viable products. How do you know this? Do some initial research. If possible, track down some of the members and customers to give you testimonial on the credibility of the program.

- The program that is catering to a growing target market. This will ensure you that there will be more and continuous demands for your referrals. Make inquiries. There are forums and discussions you can participate in to get good and reliable feedbacks.

- A program with a compensation plan that pays out a residual income and a payout of 30% or more would be a great choice. There are some programs offering this kind of compensation. Look closely for one. Do not waste your time with programs that do not reward substantially for your efforts.

- Be aware of the minimum quotas that you must fulfill or sales target that is too hard to achieve. Some affiliate programs imposes pre-requisites before you get your commissions. Just be sure that you are capable of attaining their requirements.

- Select one that has plenty of tools and resources that can help you grow the business in the shortest possible time. Not all affiliate programs have these capacities. Make use you decide on one with lots of helpful tools you can use.

- Check out if the program has a proven system that can allow you to check your networks and compensation. Also check if they have it available online for you to check anytime and anywhere.

- The program that is offering strong incentives for members to renew their membership each time. The affiliate program that provides continuous help and upgrades for its products have the tendency to retain its members. These things can assure the growth of your networks.

- Be aware of the things that members are not happy about in a program. Like with the ones mentioned above, you can do your checking at discussion forums. If you know someone in that same program, there is ho harm asking if there are many downsides involved.

Have a thorough and intensive knowledge about the affiliate program and network you will be promoting on.

Knowing the kind of program you are getting yourself into will make you anticipate and prevent any future problems you may encounter.

So Many Affiliate Programs! Which One Do I Choose?

Ask questions first before you join an affiliate program. Do a little research about the choices of program that you intend to join into. Get some answers because they will be the deciding point of what you will be achieving later on.

Will it cost you anything to join? Most affiliate programs being offered today are absolutely free of charge. So why settle for those that charge you some dollars before joining.

When do they issue the commission checks? Every program is different. Some issue their checks once a month, every quarter, etc. Select the one that is suited to your payment time choice. Many affiliate programs are setting a minimum earned commission amount that an affiliate must meet or exceed in order for their checks to be issued.

What is the hit per sale ratio? This is the average number of hits to a banner or text link it takes to generate a sale based on all affiliate statistics. This factor is extremely important because this will tell you how much traffic you must generate before you can earn a commission from the sale.

How are referrals from an affiliate's site tracked and for how long do they remain in the system? You need to be confident on the program enough to track those people you refer from your site. This is the only way that you can credit for a sale. The period of time that those people stay in the system is also important. This is because some visitors do not buy initially but may want to return later to make the purchase. Know if you will still get credit for the sale if it is done some months from a certain day.

What are the kinds of affiliate stats available? Your choice of affiliate program should be capable of offering detailed stats. They should be available online anytime you decide to check them out. Constantly checking your individual stats is important to know how many impressions, hits and sales are already generated from your site. Impressions are the number of times the banner or text link was viewed by a visitor of your site. A hit is the one clicking on the banner or text links.

Does the affiliate program also pay for the hits and impressions besides the commissions on sales? It is important that impressions and hits are also paid, as this will add to the earnings you get from the sales commission. This is especially important if the program you are in offers low sales to be able to hit ratio.

Who is the online retailer? Find out whom you are doing business with to know if it is really a solid company. Know the products they are selling and the average amount they are achieving. The more you know about the retailer offering you the affiliate program, the easier it will be for you to know if that program is really for you and your site.

Is the affiliate a one tier or two tier program? A single tier program pays you only for the business you yourself have generated. A two tier program pays you for the business, plus it also pays you a commission on the on the sales generated by any affiliate you sponsor in your program. Some two-tier programs are even paying small fees on each new affiliate you sponsor. More like a recruitment fee.

Lastly, what is the amount of commission paid? 5% - 20% is the commission paid by most programs. .01% - .05% is the amount paid for each hit. If you find a program that also pays for impressions, the amount paid is not much at all. As you can see from the figures, you will now understand why the average sales amount and hit to sale ratio is important.

These are just some of the questions that needed answering first before you enter into an affiliate program. You should be familiar with the many important aspects that your chosen program should have before incorporating them into your website. Try to ask your affiliate program choices these questions. These can help you select the right program for you site from among the many available.

Here's How To Avoid The 3 Most Common Affiliate Mistakes

Affiliate marketing is one of the most effective and powerful ways of earning some money online. This program gives everybody a chance to make a profit through the Internet. Since these affiliate marketing programs are easy to join, implement and pays a commission on a regular basis, more an more people are now willing in this business.

However, like all businesses, there are lots of pitfalls in the affiliate marketing business. Committing some of the most common mistakes will cost the marketers a large portion taken from the profit they are making everyday. That is why it is better to avoid them than be regretful in the end.

Mistake number 1: Choosing the wrong affiliate.

Many people want to earn from affiliate marketing as fast as possible. In their rush to be part of one, they tend to choose a bandwagon product. This is the kind of products that the program thinks is "hot". They choose the product that is in demand without actually considering if the product appeals to them. This is not a very wise move obviously.

Instead of jumping on the bandwagon, try top choose a product in which you are truly interested in. For any endeavor to succeed, you should take some time to plan and figure out your actions.

Pick a product that appeals to you. Then do some research about that product to see if they are in demand. Promoting a product you are more passionate about is easier than promoting one for the sake of the earnings only.

Mistake number 2: Joining too many affiliate programs.

Since affiliate programs are very easy to join, you might be tempted to join multiples of affiliate programs to try and maximize the earnings you will be getting. Besides you may think that there is nothing wrong and nothing to lose by being part of many affiliate programs.

True, that is a great way to have multiple sources of income. However, joining multiple programs and attempting to promote them all at the same time will prevent you from concentrating on each one of them.

The result? The maximum potential of your affiliate program is not realized and the income generated will not exactly be as huge as you were thinking initially it would. The best way to get excellent result is by joining just one program that pays a 40% commission at least. Then give it your best effort by promoting your products enthusiastically. As soon as you see that it is already making a reasonable profit, then maybe you can now join another affiliate program.

The technique is to do it slowly but surely. There is really no need to rush into things, especially with affiliate marketing. With the way things are going, the future is looking real bright and it seems affiliate marketing will be staying for a long time too.

Mistake number 3: Not buying the product or using the service.

As an affiliate, you main purpose is to effectively and convincingly promote a product or service and to find customers. For you to achieve this purpose, you must be able to relay to the customers that certain product and service. It is therefore difficult for you to do this when you yourself have not tried these things out. Thus, you will fail to promote and recommend them convincingly. You will also fail to create a desire in your customers to avail any of what you are offering.

Try the product or service personally first before you sign up as an affiliate to see if it is really delivering what it promises. If you have done so, then you are one of the credible and living testaments aware of its advantages and disadvantages. Your customers will then feel the sincerity and truthfulness in you and this will trigger them to try them out for themselves.

Many affiliate marketers makes these mistakes and are paying dearly for their actions. To not fall into the same situation they have been in, try to do everything to avoid making the same mistakes.

Time is the key. Take the time to analyze your marketing strategy and check if youa re in the right track. If done properly, you will be able to maximize your affiliate marketing program and earn higher profits.

Using Product Recommendations To Increase Your Bottom Line

In affiliate marketing, there are many ways in which you can increase your earnings and maintain the account that you have worked so hard for already. Most of the techniques and tactics can be learned easily. No need to go anywhere and any further. They are available online, 24 hours a day and 7 days a week.

One of the more important ways of increasing affiliate marketing bottom line and sale is through the use of product recommendations. Many marketers know that this is one of the most effective ways in promoting a certain product.

If the customers or visitors trust you enough, then they will definitely trust your recommendations. Be very careful in using this approach, though. If you start promoting everything by recommendation, your credibility will actually wear thin.

This is seen especially when recommendations are seemingly exaggerated and without much merit.

Do not be afraid to mention things that you do not like about a given product or service. Rather than lose any points for you, this will make your recommendation more realistic and will tend to increase your credibility.

Furthermore, if your visitors are really interested in what you are offering, they will be more than delighted to learn what is good about the product, what is not so good, and how the product will benefit them.

When you are recommending a certain product, there are some things to remember on how to make it work effectively and for your advantage.

Sound like the true and leading expert in your field.

Remember this simple equation: Price resistance diminishes in direct proportion to trust. If your visitors feel and believe that you are an expert in your niche, they are more inclined to making that purchase. On the other hand, if you are not exuding any confidence and self-assurance in endorsing your products, they will probably feel that same way and will go in search of another product or service which is more believable.

How do you establish this aura of expertise? By offering unique and new solutions they would not get anywhere else. Show proof that what you are promoting works as promised. Display prominent testimonials and endorsements from respected and known personalities, in related fields of course.

Avoid hype at all costs. It is better to sound low key and confident, than to scream and seek attention. Besides, you would not want to sound unprofessional and have that thinking stick to your potential customers and clients, now would you? Best to appear cool and self-assured at the same time.

And remember; prospects are not stupid. They are actually turning to experts and may already know the things that you know. If you back up your claims with hard facts and data, they would gladly put down hundreds, or even thousands worth of money to your promotions. But if you don't, they are smart enough to try and look at your competitors and what they are offering.

While recommending a product, it is also important that you give out promotional freebies. People are already familiar with the concept of offering freebies to promoting your won products. But very few people do this to promote affiliate products. Try to offer freebies that can promote or even have some information about your products or services.

Before you add recommendations to you product, it is given that you should try and test the product and support.

Do not run the risk of promoting junk products and services. Just think how long it took you to build credibility and trust among your visitors. All that will take to destroy it is one big mistake on your part.

If possible, have recommendations of products that you have 100% confidence in. Test the product support before you begin to ensure that the people you are referring it to would not be left high and dry when a problem suddenly arouse.

Have a look at your affiliate market and look at the strategies you are using. You may not be focusing on the recommendations that your products need to have. You plan of action is sometimes not the only thing that is making your program works.

Try product recommendation and be among those few who have proven its worth.

Easy Profits Using PPC In Your Affiliate Marketing Business

PPC is one of the four basic types of Search Engines. PPC is also one of the most cost-effective ways of targeted internet advertising. According to Forbes magazine, PPC or Pay Per Click, accounts to 2 billion dollars a year and is expected to increase to around 8 billion dollars by the year 2008.

Let us take a quick look at how PPC Search Engines work.

These engines create listings and rate them based on a bid amount the website owner is willing to pay for each click from that search engine. Advertisers bid against each other to receive higher ranking for a specific keyword or phrase.

The highest bidder for a certain keyword or phrase will then have the site ranked as number 1 in the PPC Search Engines followed by the second and third highest bidder, up to the last number that have placed a bid on the same keyword or phrase. Your ads then will appear prominently on the results pages based on the dollar amount bid you will agree to pay per click.

How do you make money by using PPC into your affiliate marketing business?

Most affiliate programs only pay when a sale is made or a lead delivered after a visitor has clickthrough your site. Your earnings will not always be the same as they will be dependent on the web site content and the traffic market.

The reason why you should incorporate PPC into your affiliate marketing program is that earnings are easier to make than in any other kind of affiliate program not using PPC. This way, you will be making profit based from the clickthroughs that your visitor will make on the advertiser's site. Unlike some programs, you are not paid per sale or action.

PPC can be very resourceful of your website. With PPC Search Engines incorporated into your affiliate program, you will be able to profit from the visitor's who are not interested in your products or services. The same ones who leave your site and never comes back.

You will not only get commissions not only from those who are just searching the web and finding the products and services that they wanted but you will be able to build your site's recognition as a valuable resource. The visitors who have found what they needed from you site are likely to come back and review what you are offering more closely. Then they will eventually come back to search the web for other products.

This kind of affiliate program is also an easy way for you to generate some more additional revenues. For example, when a visitor on your site does a search in the PPC Search Engine and clicks on the advertiser bided listings, the advertisers' account will then be deducted because of that click. With this, you will be compensated 30% to 80% of the advertisers' bid amount.

PPC is not only a source of generating easy profits; it can also help you promote your own site. Most of the programs allow the commissions received to be spent for advertising with them instantly and with no minimum earning requirement. This is one of the more effective ways to exchange your raw visitors for targeted surfers who has more tendencies to purchase your products and services.

What will happen if you when you integrate PPC into your affiliate program?

PPC usually have ready-to-use affiliate tools that can be easily integrated into your website. The most common tools are search boxes, banners, text links and some 404-error pages. Most search engines utilize custom solutions and can provide you with a white-label affiliate program. This enables you, using only a few lines of code, to integrate remotely-hosted co-branded search engine into your website.

The key benefits? Not only more money generated but also some extra money on the side. Plus a lifetime commissions once you have referred some webmaster friends to the engine.

Think about it. Where can you get all these benefits while already generating some income for your site? Knowing some of the more useful tools you can use for your affiliate program is not a waste of time. They are rather a means of earning within an earning.

Best know more about how you can use PPC search engines into your affiliate program than miss out on a great opportunity to earn more profits.

Using Camtasia Can Increase Your Affiliate Checks

Since there are already lots of people getting into affiliate marketing, it is no wonder that the competition is getting stiff. The challenge is to try and outdo other affiliates and think of ways to be able to attain this.

There are also many tips and techniques being taught to these affiliate in order to best plan their strategy for their program to work effectively so that more earnings will be achieved.

What better way to wow your prospects and customers than to record and publish top notch, full motion and streaming screen-captured videos. Nothing like feeling your hard work getting paid by having your customers jumping up excitedly in great anticipation to buy your product right there and then.

This is Camtasia in action. It is a proven fact; giving your customers something they can actually see can explode your online sales instantly.

You do not need to have training and education to be able to know how this system can work for your affiliate program. Anyone can create stunning videos, from multimedia tutorials and step-by-step presentations available online. The process is like having your customers seated next to you and looking at your desktop, as you show them the things they need to see and hear. All this done step by step.

For those who does not know it yet, how does Camtasia works?

- It can record your desktop activity in a single click. No need to have to save and compile all your files because it is recorded right there and then.

- Can easily convert your videos into web pages. Once converted you can have your customers visiting that certain page. Videos are easier to understand and take in unlike reading texts which oftentimes is a trying thing to do.

- Upload your pages. Publish them through blogs, RSS feed and podcasts. You may want your Camtasis videos to get around and reach out to other people that may be potential customers in the future. Nothing like being visible in many sites and pages to advertise yourself and get your message through.

There are other things you can do with your affiliate program using Camtasia. You can...

Create stunning multimedia presentations that are proven to increase sales because all the senses are engaged. This also has the tendency to reduce skepticism among hard-to-please customers.

Reduce refunds and other customer issues by demonstrating visually how to use your product and how to do it properly. Complaints will also be minimized because all the facts and the presentation are there for the customers to just see and hear about.

Promote affiliate products and services using visual presentations. This is an effective way of redirecting your viewers straight to your affiliate website after they are finished with the video. Make the most of the presentation by putting your site location in the end and make them go there directly if they want more information.

Multiple your online auction bids exponentially when you give your readers a feel of what you have to offer. Based from reports, auctions that includes pictures increases bidding percentage by 400%. Imagine how much higher it will be if it were videos.

Publish valuable infoproducts that you can sell for a much higher price. It will be all worth the price because of the full colored graphics menu and templates that you will be using.

Minimize miscommunication with your customers. Instantly showing them what you want they wanted in the first place is making them understand clearly the essence of your affiliate program. The good thing about multimedia is, nothing much can go wrong. It is there already.

These are just some of the things you can do with Camtasia that can be very helpful in your chosen affiliate program.

Note that the main purpose of using Camtasia is to boost the income that is generated from your affiliate program. Although it can be used for entertainment and enjoyment purposes, which is not really a valid reason why you choose to get all through that trouble.

Try to focus on the goal that you have set upon yourself to and achieve that with the use of the things that may be quite a lot of help in increasing your earnings.

How To Become A Super Affiliate In Niche Markets

Over the past years, web hosting has grown bigger than it used to be. With more companies getting into this business and finding the many benefits it can give them, the demand for web hosting has never been higher. These seem to be the trend of today.

38 million people have put up their very first websites online this year 2005 alone. It is estimated that by 2008, the internet sales industry will top then dollar bank. And to think, majority of those sites will be offering different affiliate programs for people to choose and participate into.

This only means one thing. It is easier now to find the right web host for your application. The possibility of quality web hosting companies separating themselves from the rest of the industry is anticipated. If this is done, the unprofessional and incompetent ones will suffer.

Support will be the number one consideration for people when choosing a web host. It will be obvious that traditional advertising will become less and less effective. Most people would rather opt for the web host based on things that they see and hear. Also based on the recommendations by those who have tried them and have proved to be a successful.

This is a great opportunity for web hosting affiliates and resellers alike. There would hundreds of web hosting and programs to choose from that the difficulty in finding the right one for them is not a problem anymore.

How does one become a successful affiliate in the niche markets using web hosting?

If you think about it, everyone who needs a website needs a web hosting company to host it for them. As of now, there is really no leading hosting industry so most people choose hosts based from recommendations. Usually, they get it from the ones that have already availed of a web hosting services.

With the many hosts offering affiliate programs, there is the tendency to find the one which you think will work best for you. Think of the product you will be promoting. Pattern them to the site and see if they are catering to the same things as you are.

When you have been with one host for quite some time and seem not to be making much despite all your effort, leave that one and look for another. There is no use in trying to stick to one when you would be before off in another one. Things will only have to get better from there because you already have been in worst situations.

Try this out. If you are quite happy and satisfied with your web host, try to see if they are offering an affiliate program you can participate on. Instead of you paying them, why not make it the other way around; them paying you. The process can be as easy as putting a small "powered by" or "hosted by" link at the bottom of your page and you are already in an affiliate business.

Why choose paying for your for your web hosting when you do not have to? Try to get paid by letting people know you like your web host.

Always remember that when choosing a web host, choose the one that is known for its fantastic customer support. There are also many hosting affiliate programs. Residual affiliate program is also being hosted. This is the program wherein you get paid a percentage every month for a client that you refer. This can allow you to have a steady source of income. With perseverance, you can even be quite successful in this field.

There are a lot of niche markets out there just waiting for the right affiliate to penetrate to them and make that dollars dream come true. Knowing which one to get into is being confident enough of your potentials and the good results you will be getting.

Web hosting is just one affiliate market you could try out and make some good and continuous income. Just remember that to be successful on your endeavor also means that time, effort and patience is needed.

Nobody has invented the perfect affiliate market yet. But some people do know how to make it big in this kind of market. It is just knowing your kind of market and making the earnings there.

Bonus

Get Related Materials

from Our Free Library

Instant Access – Join Here

Click or type into your browser:

http://livesensical.com/go/byob/

www.ingramcontent.com/pod-product-compliance
Lightning Source LLC
Chambersburg PA
CBHW030012190526
45157CB00015B/2458